# Starting from Scratch

# Starting from Scratch

## Cooking and Entertaining Made Simple

by Merle Rosenbloom

*When Life
Hands You Lemons,
Use Them
as Garnish.*

Anonymous

# Contents

## *Settings Simplified*

# Introduction

*Starting from Scratch: Cooking and Entertaining Made Simple* is the culmination of my journey toward being an excellent cook and entertainer. My husband, Brian, to whom I've been married since I was nineteen, is my biggest cheerleader, but he used to affectionately joke that I "burnt the salad." With his encouragement and my voracious appetite to improve, I began doing the opposite of what seemed natural: entertaining as much as I had time for and attending as many cooking classes as I could find. My Cuisinart was my best friend in those early years because, with my job at an attorney's office, time was limited. Despite my full schedule, I savored my weekends, which were spent hosting dinner parties that were known for their beautiful tablescapes and delicious food.

I immigrated from South Africa to the United States in the 1980s, bringing my love for entertaining and food with me. I opened a food-basket business and later a successful catering company.

Fast forward several years, a friend asked me to host a cooking class for her and her newlywed friends. I obliged and continued those lessons for years. The rest, as they say, is history. *Starting from Scratch* began as a simple collection of my favorite recipes, bound in a book for my daughter-in-law as a bridal shower gift, but the requests for copies poured in. Despite a multiple myeloma* diagnosis and a few year hiatus, my heart has always been in taking my original cookbook to the next level. This book is a can't-miss reference for any novice in the kitchen who is inspired to learn to create delicious meals and be the exceptional host. The recipes inside are a carefully curated collection of my favorites from over the years.

Congratulations on taking the first step on your own culinary journey. I hope that *Starting from Scratch: Cooking and Entertaining Made Simple* leads you to a lifetime of unforgettable memories around the table.

* A portion of the proceeds from the sale of this cookbook will go toward multiple myeloma research.

KAME
Ginger
Tart Cherries
Lieber's
Onion Soup mix
Hidden Valley
Dips
Ranch
Uncle Ben's
Ready
Whole Grain Medley

# Simple Selections

Whether you're a master chef or beginner cook, the same rule applies: preparation is everything. Read the recipe, make your grocery list, and shop smart. Save time by preparing your ingredients ahead of time and measuring everything out. Some menu items can be made a day or two in advance. Your table décor and floral arrangements may be completed in advance, too. Don't strive for perfection but aim to entertain in a way that makes you proud.

# Kitchen Essentials

The importance of quality kitchen utensils is paramount in your journey to becoming a great cook and entertainer. Equipment like nonstick pans, measuring utensils, sharp knives, kitchen scissors, and my old friend the Cuisinart makes your job that much easier.

**STOVETOP**

Clockwise from Bottom Left: 10-Inch Fry Pan with 3-Quart Sauté Pan with Lid inside, 8-Inch Fry Pan with 1½-Quart Saucepan with Lid inside, 8-Quart Stockpot with Lid, 3-Quart Sauté Pan with Lid

## Baking

Clockwise from Top Left:
Large Baking Sheet,
9×9-Inch Metal Baking Pan
8×8-Inch Glass
Baking Dish,
Nonstick 12-Count
Muffin/Cupcake Pan,
9-Inch Round
Baking Pan,
Small Baking Sheet,
Ramekins, Loaf Pan,
Bundt Pan,
9-Inch Pie Plate

## Prep

Left to Right/Top to Bottom:
Colander,
Set of Measuring Spoons,
Peppermill,
Set of Measuring Cups,
2-Cup Glass Measuring Cup,
Set of 3 Mixing Bowls, Grater

## KNIVES/CHOPPING

Top to Bottom:
Wood Cutting Board,
Vegetable Peeler,
Boning Knife,
Paring Knife,
Plastic Cutting Board

## UTENSILS

Left to Right:
Rubber Spatula,
Wire Whisk,
Basting Brush,
Large Slotted Spoon,
Ladle,
3 Wooden Spoons,
Kitchen Shears,
Can Opener,
Rubber Spatula,
Metal Tongs

**SMALL APPLIANCES**

Clockwise from Left: Electric Hand Mixer, Timer, Hand Blender, Food Processor, Scale

# Pantry Essentials

A great entertainer always has a well-stocked pantry with essentials that make it simple to create recipes on the fly. All of these items can be found in your local grocery store, so you are spared the trip to a gourmet market.

**BAKING NEEDS**

Front: Brown Sugar, Baking Powder, Vanilla Extract, Sugar
Back: All-Purpose Flour, Powdered Sugar, Self-Rising Flour

**PASTA –** Clockwise from Top Left: Angel Hair, Spaghetti, Fettuccine, Penne Rigate

**NUTS AND SEEDS –** Left to Right: Pecans, Walnuts, Almonds, Sesame Seeds

**RICE –** Top to Bottom: Brown Rice, Long Grain Rice, Rice Blend; Other Essential: Wild Rice

## Herbs and Spices

Left to Right: Parsley, Cinnamon, Basil, Paprika, Thyme, Sesame Seeds, Cayenne Pepper, Rosemary, Ginger, Oregano; Other Essentials: Salt, Black Peppercorns, White Pepper, Mixed Herbs, Chili Powder, Curry Powder, Bay Leaves, Nutmeg, Garlic Salt, Onion Salt, Chicken Seasoning, Chicken Bouillon Cubes, Beef Bouillon Cubes, Chunky Garlic Stir-In Paste, Chef Paul Prudhomme's Magic Seasoning Blends – Meat Magic

## Canned Goods

Left to Right: Whole Kernel Corn, Artichokes, Asparagus Spears, Whole Peeled Tomatoes; Other Essentials: Tomato Purée, Tomato Paste, Asparagus Cuts, Tuna, Salmon, Anchovies, Sliced Peaches, Apricot Jam, Strawberry Jam

**CONDIMENTS –** Left to Right: Worcestershire Sauce, Soy Sauce, Dijon Mustard, Ketchup, Coarse Ground Mustard, Balsamic Vinegar; Other Essential: Dale's Steak Seasoning

## OILS AND VINEGARS

Left to Right: Rice Vinegar, Canola Oil, White Wine Vinegar, Red Wine Vinegar, Extra-Virgin Olive Oil; Other Essential: Nonstick Cooking Spray

## LIQUORS

Left to Right: Chardonnay, Brandy, Dry Sherry, Cabernet Sauvignon

1 teaspoon (5 ml)
1/4 teaspoon (1.25 ml)
UNIT
7Kgx1g

# Measurement Equivalents

| Cup | Fluid Ounces | Tablespoons | Teaspoons | Milliliters |
|---|---|---|---|---|
| 1 | 8 | 16 | 48 | 237 |
| 3/4 | 6 | 12 | 36 | 177 |
| 2/3 | 5 | 11 | 32 | 158 |
| 1/2 | 4 | 8 | 24 | 118 |
| 1/3 | 3 | 5 | 16 | 79 |
| 1/4 | 2 | 4 | 12 | 59 |
| 1/8 | 1 | 2 | 6 | 30 |
| 1/16 | 1/2 | 1 | 3 | 15 |

# Simply Savor

Savor doesn't just apply to a delicious meal. During your preparation, ensure that you aren't creating added stress. Enjoy the art of setting your table.

A delicious meal has the ability to send us to far-off exotic places, bring about memories forgotten over time, and evoke feelings otherwise lost in translation. As we explore new foods, the tastes, textures, and aromas can transport us. Few things are as fulfilling as savoring your hard work as your friends and family relish the fruits of your labor.

*Pesto Torta*

# Appetizers

# Baked Crab Dip

**Serves 8 to 10**

**12 to 14 ounces imitation or fresh crabmeat, chopped**
**1/2 cup mayonnaise**
**7 teaspoons drained capers**
**2 1/2 teaspoons prepared horseradish**
**1 tablespoon Tabasco sauce**
**1 tablespoon Worcestershire sauce**
**2/3 cup grated mild cheddar cheese**

Preheat the oven to 350 degrees.

Combine the crabmeat, mayonnaise, capers, horseradish, Tabasco sauce and Worcestershire sauce in a bowl and mix well. Spoon into a baking dish and sprinkle with the cheese.

Bake for 20 minutes. Place the dish 6 inches from the heat source. Broil for 2 minutes or until golden brown and bubbly. Serve with a mixture of crackers.

# Salmon Mousse

**Serves 8 to 10**

**1 envelope unflavored gelatin**
**1/4 cup cold water**
**1/4 cup boiling water**
**2 (6-ounce) cans red or pink salmon**
**1 cup mayonnaise**
**1/4 cup sour cream**
**1 onion, finely chopped**
**2 tablespoons lemon juice**
**2 teaspoons dill weed**
**1 teaspoon salt**
**1 teaspoon paprika**

Soften the gelatin in the cold water in a large bowl. Add the boiling water and stir until dissolved.

Drain the salmon. Add the salmon, mayonnaise, sour cream, onion, lemon juice, dill weed, salt and paprika to the gelatin and mix well.

Spray a fish mold or small glass bowl with nonstick spray. Pour the mixture into the mold and chill overnight. Unmold onto a serving plate or serve from the bowl. Serve with crackers or cocktail rye bread.

# Layered Smoked Salmon Pâté

**Serves 10 to 12**

2 to 3 avocados
Lemon juice to taste
1 pound smoked salmon
16 ounces cream cheese, softened
Freshly ground black pepper to taste
3 tablespoons drained capers
1 small red onion, chopped
3 tablespoons chopped fresh chives

*Tip: Place an unpeeled avocado in boiling water for 1 minute to keep it from browning after it is peeled.*

Line a small loaf pan with plastic wrap.

Mash the avocados in a bowl. Stir in the lemon juice.

Layer a fourth of the salmon, half the cream cheese, a fourth of the salmon and half the avocados in the prepared loaf pan. Sprinkle with pepper. Layer with half the capers and onion.

Layer with a fourth of the salmon and remaining half of the cream cheese. Sprinkle with pepper. Layer with remaining halves of the capers, onion and avocados.

Top with the remaining fourth of the salmon. Place a sheet of plastic wrap on top of the pâté and press lightly to compact. Refrigerate for at least 3 hours.

Remove the plastic wrap and invert the pâté onto a serving plate, removing the remaining plastic wrap. Sprinkle with the chives. Serve with mini bagels, bagel chips or cocktail rye bread.

# Baked Brie with Chutney

**Serves 8 to 10**

**1 sheet frozen puff pastry, thawed**
**1 (5-inch) round brie cheese**
**Salt and pepper to taste**
**1 egg, lightly beaten**
**1 cup chutney, any flavor**

Tip: *Any flavor of soft jam may be substituted for the chutney.*

Preheat the oven to 400 degrees. Line a baking sheet with parchment paper.

Roll the pastry out on a floured surface. Cut a 12-inch circle from the dough. Place the brie in the center of the circle and sprinkle with salt and pepper. Wrap the pastry around the cheese to enclose, sealing seams. Place on the prepared baking sheet.

Cut decorations out of the dough scraps using a paring knife or small cookie cutters. Arrange on top of the wrapped brie. Brush with the egg.

Bake for 20 minutes or until golden brown. Reduce the oven temperature to 325 degrees. Bake for 20 minutes longer. Let stand to cool for 5 to 10 minutes. Transfer to a plate using the parchment paper. Serve with a side of chutney and sliced vegetables, apples and baguette.

# Pesto Torta

**Serves 8**

**4 fresh basil leaves**
**4 sun-dried tomatoes**
**18 ounces garlic-and-herb spreadable cheese, at room temperature**
**1/4 cup bottled sun-dried tomato tapenade**
**1/4 cup basil pesto**

Line a 3-cup bowl with plastic wrap. Spray the plastic wrap with nonstick spray.

Arrange the basil leaves and sun-dried tomatoes in a decorative pattern in the bottom of the prepared bowl. Spread with half the cheese, all of the tomato tapenade and all of the basil pesto. Spread the remaining cheese over the top of the pesto and press firmly. Chill, covered, for 3 to 4 hours.

Invert the torta onto a serving plate and remove the plastic wrap. Serve with baguette slices and sliced fresh vegetables of your choice.

*Pictured on page 24*

# Tortilla Stack

**Serves 6 to 8**

- 1 large onion, thinly sliced
- 2 jalapeño chiles, seeded and finely sliced
- 2 tablespoons butter
- 6 to 8 tortillas
- Bottled sweet chili sauce or chutney
- 8 ounces brie cheese, thinly sliced
- 2 mangos, peeled and cut into strips (optional)
- Chopped fresh cilantro to taste
- 1 cup grated mild or sharp cheddar cheese

Preheat the oven to 400 degrees. Grease a baking sheet.

Sauté the onion and jalapeños with the butter in a skillet over medium heat for 5 to 7 minutes or until tender.

Place 1 tortilla on a work surface and spread thinly with chili sauce. Layer thinly with brie, onion mixture, mangos, cilantro and cheddar cheese. Repeat layers until all of the ingredients are used, ending with a tortilla; press lightly. Transfer the stack to the prepared baking sheet.

Bake for 8 to 10 minutes or until heated through. Let stand for 5 minutes. Cut into wedges with a pizza cutter.

# Asparagus Quiche

Serves 4 to 6

- 3 eggs
- 1/2 cup milk
- 2 (14-ounce) cans asparagus cuts, drained
- 1 onion, grated
- 16 ounces grated sharp cheddar cheese
- 1/4 cup minced fresh parsley
- Salt and pepper to taste
- Poppy seeds

Preheat the oven to 425 degrees. Spray a 9 × 9-inch baking dish with nonstick cooking spray.

Beat the eggs and milk in a large bowl. Add the asparagus, onion, cheese, parsley, salt and pepper and mix well.

Spoon the mixture into the prepared baking dish. Sprinkle poppy seeds over the top. Bake for 20 minutes. Serve immediately.

# Stuffed Loaf with Asparagus and Mushrooms

Serves 8 to 10

- 1 loaf French bread
- 2 (14-ounce) cans asparagus cuts, well drained
- 1 (4-ounce) can sliced mushrooms, well drained
- 1/4 cup mayonnaise
- 2 tablespoons dijon mustard
- Cayenne pepper to taste
- 1 cup finely shredded medium cheddar cheese (optional)

Preheat the oven to 350 degrees. Cut a slit lengthwise down the center of the bread. Hollow out the bread, leaving a 1/2-inch shell.

Combine the asparagus, mushrooms, mayonnaise, mustard and cayenne pepper in a bowl and mix well.

Fill the bread shell with the asparagus mixture; sprinkle with the cheese. Wrap in foil. Bake for 25 minutes. Remove from the foil and place on a serving platter. Slice on the diagonal to serve.

# Artichoke Spinach Dip

**Serves 8 to 10**

**1 (15-ounce) can artichoke hearts**
**5 ounces frozen spinach, thawed**
**1 1/2 cups part-skim ricotta cheese**
**1 teaspoon grated lemon zest**
**1 teaspoon fresh thyme leaves**
**2 garlic cloves, minced**
**1 teaspoon kosher salt**
**1/8 teaspoon cayenne pepper**
**1/4 cup grated parmesan cheese**
**1/2 cup panko bread crumbs**

Tip: *Chunky garlic stir-in paste works well in place of the minced garlic. It is located with the herbs in the refrigerator section of your local grocery store.*

Preheat the oven to 350 degrees. Spray a 4-cup baking dish with nonstick cooking spray.

Drain the artichokes and spinach, pressing well to remove any excess liquid.

Combine the ricotta cheese, lemon zest, thyme, garlic, salt and cayenne pepper in a food processor and blend until smooth. Add the artichokes, spinach and parmesan cheese. Pulse until mixed but still chunky.

Spoon the dip into the prepared baking dish. Sprinkle with the bread crumbs. Bake for 20 to 30 minutes or until hot and bubbly. Serve with crackers.

# Avocado Dip

**Serves 4 to 6**

2 ripe avocados
6 ounces cream cheese
1/2 cup sour cream
1/2 cup mayonnaise
3 tablespoons lemon juice
2 tablespoons vinegar
1/2 teaspoon dijon mustard
1/2 teaspoon salt
1/8 teaspoon Tabasco sauce

Blend the avocados, cream cheese, sour cream, mayonnaise, lemon juice, vinegar, mustard, salt and Tabasco sauce in a blender until smooth. Suggested serving options include potato chips, carrot sticks, sliced mushrooms, radishes and celery sticks.

# Sun-Dried Tomato Hummus

**Serves 10 to 12**

1 package whole wheat pita bread rounds
1 jar oil-pack sun-dried tomatoes
1 1/2 cups chickpeas, rinsed and drained
3/4 cup cannelloni beans, rinsed and drained
1 small garlic clove, peeled
1/4 cup plain nonfat yogurt
2 tablespoons fresh lemon juice
1/2 teaspoon toasted sesame seed oil
1/4 teaspoon ground cumin
1/4 teaspoon salt

Preheat the oven to 350 degrees.

Cut each pita into fourths and arrange on a baking sheet. Bake for 10 minutes.

Drain 1 tablespoon oil from the sun-dried tomatoes and reserve. Purée the chickpeas, cannelloni beans, 8 sun-dried tomatoes, reserved oil and garlic in a food processor. Add the yogurt, lemon juice, sesame seed oil, cumin and salt. Blend until smooth.

Pour into a serving bowl. Serve with the toasted pitas and sliced fresh vegetables.

# Mini Cheese and Olive Calzones

**Serves 8**

**1/2 cup ricotta cheese**
**1/4 cup shredded Mexican-blend cheese**
**1/4 cup chopped black olives**
**1 teaspoon Italian seasoning**
**1 (8-ounce) can crescent dinner rolls**

Preheat the oven to 375 degrees. Spray a baking sheet with nonstick cooking spray.

Combine the ricotta cheese, Mexican-blend cheese, black olives and Italian seasoning in a medium bowl and mix well.

Unroll the crescent dough and roll out into a 16×18-inch rectangle on a floured surface. Cut into 8 squares using a pizza cutter.

Spoon 2 tablespoons of cheese filling onto each square. Moisten the edges of the squares lightly with water. Fold the dough over the filling and seal using a fork. Pierce the top of each calzone twice using a fork.

Arrange on the prepared baking sheet. Bake for 20 minutes. Serve hot.

# Hot Mexican-Style Spinach Dip

**Serves 6 to 8**

1 (10-ounce) can tomatoes and green chilies
2 cups shredded Monterey Jack cheese
8 ounces cream cheese, cut into small pieces
1/2 cup half-and-half
2 (2-ounce) cans sliced black olives, drained (about 1 cup)
1 tablespoon red wine vinegar
1 (10-ounce) package frozen spinach, thawed and squeezed dry
Salt and freshly ground black pepper to taste

Preheat the oven to 400 degrees.

Combine the tomatoes and green chilies, Monterey Jack cheese, cream cheese, half-and-half, black olives and vinegar in a large bowl and mix well. Add the spinach, salt and pepper and mix well.

Spoon into 3 (.25 qt.) ramekins. Bake for 20 minutes or until hot and bubbly and the top is golden brown. Garnish with torn fresh cilantro. Serve with tortilla chips.

*Tip: You may spoon the dip into an 8×8-inch baking dish instead of the ramekins and bake for 35 minutes.*

*Skinny Chopped Vegetable Salad*

# Salads

# Arugula Salad with Strawberries

**Serves 4 to 6**

1/2 pint strawberries, quartered
2 tablespoons balsamic vinegar
2 tablespoons olive oil
1/4 teaspoon salt
1/4 teaspoon pepper
2 (5-ounce) packages arugula
1/2 cup pecans, toasted
Crumbled feta cheese (optional)

Place the strawberries in a large bowl. Drizzle with 1 tablespoon vinegar and stir gently. Let stand for 5 to 10 minutes.

Whisk the olive oil, remaining 1 tablespoon vinegar, salt and pepper in a small bowl.

Add the arugula to the strawberries. Drizzle with the vinaigrette and toss to mix. Add the pecans and cheese and toss gently. Serve immediately.

# Goat Cheese Salad with Mustard Dressing

Serves 4

1 head butter lettuce
1 head radicchio
1 small bunch watercress
1 small bunch endive
8 ounces goat cheese
Mustard Dressing

Separate the butter lettuce, radicchio, watercress and endive leaves and arrange on a serving platter. Crumble the cheese over the salad. Cover and refrigerate until serving time. Drizzle with the Mustard Dressing just before serving.

## Mustard Dressing

3 tablespoons olive oil
1 tablespoon white vinegar
2 teaspoons French mustard
1/2 teaspoon finely chopped fresh basil leaves

Combine the olive oil, vinegar, mustard and basil in a small bowl and whisk to mix well.

# Spinach Salad with Poppy Seed Dressing

**Serves 4 to 6**

1 pound small white mushrooms
3 tablespoons light olive oil
Salt and pepper to taste
10 ounces spinach
1 large head butter lettuce
2 eggs, hard-boiled and chopped
1 red onion, thinly sliced
1/3 cup pine nuts, toasted
1 avocado, sliced
Poppy Seed Dressing

Sauté the mushrooms with the olive oil until the oil is absorbed, seasoning with salt and pepper while cooking. Let stand to cool.

Combine the spinach, butter lettuce, eggs, onion, pine nuts and mushrooms in a large bowl. Cover and refrigerate until serving time. Add the avocado and toss with the Poppy Seed Dressing just before serving.

## Poppy Seed Dressing

1/2 cup fresh orange juice
1/2 cup olive oil
1/3 cup white wine vinegar
1/4 cup mayonnaise
1 tablespoon poppy seeds
1 teaspoon salt
1/2 teaspoon sugar
Freshly ground black pepper to taste

Combine the orange juice, olive oil, vinegar, mayonnaise, poppy seeds, salt, sugar and pepper in a bowl and whisk to mix well. Dressing may be refrigerated for up to 4 days before using.

*Tip: Place thinly sliced red onions in ice water for about 15 minutes to reduce the pungent taste.*

# Spinach Salad with Apricot Vinaigrette

Serves 4

10 ounces baby spinach
1 pint cherry or grape tomatoes
1 small red onion, thinly sliced
1/2 cup chopped dried apricots
4 ounces goat cheese, crumbled
1 avocado, diced
1/4 cup chopped pecans, toasted
Apricot Vinaigrette

Combine the spinach, tomatoes, onion, dried apricots, cheese, avocado and pecans in a large bowl. Toss with the Apricot Vinaigrette just before serving.

## Apricot Vinaigrette

1/2 cup vegetable oil
2 tablespoons white wine vinegar
2 tablespoons orange juice
2 tablespoons apricot jam
1/2 teaspoon salt
1/2 teaspoon ground coriander
1/2 teaspoon freshly ground pepper

Combine the vegetable oil, vinegar, orange juice, apricot jam, salt, coriander and pepper in a small bowl and whisk to mix well.

# Cabbage and Tomato Slaw with Sherry Vinaigrette

Serves 8

12 cups thinly sliced cabbage
12 ounces grape or cherry tomatoes, cut into halves
10 green onions, thinly sliced (bulb removed)
Sherry Vinaigrette
Salt and pepper to taste

Combine the cabbage, tomatoes and green onions in a large bowl. Add the Sherry Vinaigrette and toss well. Season with salt and pepper. Cover and refrigerate for 2 to 4 hours. Toss before serving.

## Sherry Vinaigrette

1/3 cup sherry wine vinegar
3 tablespoons honey
2 tablespoons mustard seeds
2/3 cup olive oil

Combine the vinegar, honey and mustard seeds in a small bowl and whisk to mix well. Add the olive oil gradually, whisking constantly until well blended.

*Tip: For a time-saver, use prepackaged chopped cabbage.*

# Cabbage Salad

**Serves 4 to 6**

3/4 cup chopped walnuts or pecans
3/4 cup pine nuts or sliced almonds
1/2 cup sesame seeds
1 bunch green onions, thinly sliced
2 (10-ounce) package shredded cabbage
Soy Vinaigrette

Spray a skillet with nonstick cooking spray. Toast the walnuts, pine nuts and sesame seeds in the skillet over medium-high heat. Let stand to cool.

Reserve 2 tablespoons green onions for garnish. Combine the cabbage, remaining green onions, walnut mixture and Soy Vinaigrette in a large bowl and toss well. Garnish with the reserved green onions. Let stand for 15 minutes before serving.

## Soy Vinaigrette

1/2 cup white vinegar
1/4 cup vegetable oil
1/4 cup sugar
1/2 tablespoon soy sauce

Combine the vinegar, vegetable oil, sugar and soy sauce in a small bowl and whisk to mix well.

*Tip: Thinly sliced fresh or prepackaged angel hair cabbage works well with any color combination of cabbage. Use the combination of any two types of nuts that suits your taste.*

# Kale Salad

**Serves 10 to 12**

1 (10-ounce) package kale or baby kale
1 (10-ounce) package shaved brussels sprouts
1 (10-ounce) package spinach
1 (10-ounce) package butter lettuce
1 (10-ounce) package spring mix
1/2 cup baby tomatoes
1/2 cup chopped cucumber
1/2 cup dried cranberries
1 cup walnut or pecan halves
Bottled champagne vinaigrette, or Poppy Seed Dressing (recipe on page 44)

*Tip: Make this salad your own by adding whatever vegetables you wish.*

Combine the kale, brussels sprouts, spinach, butter lettuce, spring mix, tomatoes and cucumber in a large bowl.

Sprinkle the dried cranberries and walnuts over the salad. Dress with the desired amount of champagne vinaigrette just before serving.

# Skinny Chopped Vegetable Salad

**Serves 6**

$^1/_2$ bunch asparagus
Olive oil
Kosher salt to taste
1 red bell pepper, chopped
1 yellow bell pepper, chopped
1 poblano pepper, chopped
1 jalapeño chile, chopped (optional)
1 pint cherry tomatoes, cut into halves
2 or 3 ribs celery, chopped
$^1/_4$ to $^1/_2$ cup chopped red onion
$^1/_2$ English cucumber, chopped
Chopped fresh parsley
Chopped fresh cilantro
1 avocado
Salad dressing

Preheat the oven to 400 degrees.

Arrange the asparagus on a baking sheet. Drizzle with olive oil and season with salt. Roast for 3 minutes or just until crisp and tender.

Combine the asparagus, red bell pepper, yellow bell pepper, poblano pepper, jalapeño, tomatoes, celery, onion, cucumber, parsley and cilantro in a large bowl and mix well.

Cut the avocado into bite-size pieces and add to the salad immediately before serving. Toss with the dressing of your choice.

*pictured on page 40*

# Tomato, Mozzarella and Basil Salad

**Serves 8 to 10**

**3 large firm tomatoes, sliced**
**2 fresh mozzarella cheese logs, sliced**
**Black peppercorns to taste**
**1 bunch fresh basil leaves**
**1/4 cup balsamic vinegar**
**1/4 cup olive oil**

*Tip: Cucumber and avocado slices may be added to the salad.*

Arrange the tomatoes and cheese in alternating slices on a large decorative platter. Grind pepper over the top.

Chop half the basil leaves. Sprinkle whole and chopped basil leaves over the tomatoes and cheese.

Combine the balsamic vinegar and olive oil in a bowl and whisk to mix well. Drizzle over the salad.

# Soups

*Butternut Squash Soup*

# Lobster Bisque

**Serves 4 to 6**

1 (1-pound) lobster, cut into 1-inch pieces
1/2 medium white onion
1/4 cup distilled white vinegar
Salt and pepper to taste
1 (10-ounce) can tomato soup
1 (10-ounce) can green pea soup
10 ounces water
10 ounces heavy cream
1/4 cup dry sherry

Combine the lobster, onion, vinegar, salt and pepper in a saucepan. Add just enough water to cover. Bring to a boil. Boil for 10 to 15 minutes. Remove the lobster to a plate. Let stand to cool; drain any excess liquid.

Combine the tomato soup, pea soup and 10 ounces water in a saucepan over low heat. Cook until heated through, stirring occasionally. Add the cream gradually, stirring constantly.

Add the lobster and sherry to the soup mixture. Cook until heated through, stirring frequently; do not boil. Ladle into soup bowls.

# Vegetable Soup

**Serves 10 to 12**

- 3 (10-ounce) packages frozen soup vegetables or mixed vegetables
- 1 package frozen sliced carrots
- 3 (32-ounce) boxes low-sodium chicken broth
- Salt and pepper to taste

Combine the soup vegetables, carrots and chicken broth in a stockpot. Bring to a boil over medium-high heat. Reduce the heat to low. Simmer for 1 hour, stirring occasionally. Let stand to cool slightly.

Purée in batches in a blender, pouring batches into a large bowl. Return the soup to the stockpot. Season with salt and pepper. Reheat the soup and ladle into soup bowls. Serve with hot French bread or crusty rolls.

*Tip: This soup can be frozen for 3 months or refrigerated for up to 5 days.*

# Gazpacho

Serves 10 to 12

8 plum tomatoes
2 unpeeled English cucumbers, halved and seeded
3 red bell peppers, cored and seeded
2 red onions
6 garlic cloves, finely chopped
46 ounces tomato juice
1/2 cup white wine vinegar
1/2 cup olive oil
1 tablespoon kosher salt
1 1/2 teaspoons freshly ground pepper

Cut the tomatoes, cucumbers, bell peppers and onions into 1-inch pieces. Process the tomatoes in a food processor or pulse in a blender until coarsely chopped; do not overprocess. Spoon into a large bowl. Repeat the process with the cucumbers, bell peppers and onions. Add the garlic, tomato juice, vinegar, olive oil, salt and pepper and mix well.

Chill, covered, overnight. Ladle into soup bowls. Garnish with parsley. Serve with fresh celery sticks.

*Tip: The longer this soup sits in the refrigerator, the more the flavors develop. To add a little kick, add 1 or 2 chopped jalapeño chiles or 1 tablespoon Tabasco sauce. The recipe can be cut in half.*

# Fresh Mushroom Soup

**Serves 6**

3 pounds fresh mushrooms, sliced
4 tablespoons butter
1 tablespoon lemon juice
2 tablespoons all-purpose flour
1 (32-ounce) box vegetable broth
4 egg yolks
1/4 cup dry sherry
Salt and pepper to taste

*Tip: Do not wash mushrooms; they absorb water. Simply clean them with a paper towel.*

Sauté the mushrooms with the butter in a skillet for 5 minutes. Sprinkle with the lemon juice. Stir in the flour. Add the vegetable broth and mix well. Bring to a boil, stirring constantly.

Beat the egg yolks and sherry in a small bowl. Add 1/2 cup of the mushroom mixture and mix well. Add to the remaining mushroom mixture. Season with salt and pepper. Cook until heated through, stirring frequently; do not boil. Ladle into soup bowls.

# Butternut Squash Soup

**Serves 8**

1 large onion, chopped
3 tablespoons butter
2 pounds butternut squash,
  peeled and cubed
2 apples, peeled and cubed
2 cups vegetable broth
1/2 cup apple cider
1 teaspoon ground ginger
1/4 cup heavy cream
1/2 teaspoon salt
Pepper to taste

Sauté the onion with the butter in a skillet over medium heat for 5 to 7 minutes or until tender. Stir in the squash, apples, vegetable broth, apple cider and ginger. Cook over low heat for 25 minutes or longer. Pour into a blender. Blend until smooth, thinning with additional broth if needed.

Stir in the heavy cream and season with the salt and pepper just before serving. Ladle into soup bowls. Garnish with whipped cream and pumpkin seeds.

*pictured on page 55*

# Parmesan Croutons

**Makes 24**

1 baguette
$^{1}/_{4}$ cup olive oil
Kosher or sea salt to taste
Freshly ground black pepper to taste
1 cup grated parmesan cheese

Preheat the oven to 400 degrees. Cut the bread diagonally into $^{1}/_{2}$-inch slices.

Arrange the slices in a single layer on a baking sheet. Brush with the olive oil and sprinkle with salt and pepper. Top with the cheese.

Bake for 12 minutes. Let stand to cool.

*Tip: These croutons are great for use in any hot soup or as a side with a salad.*

# Meats

*Meat Loaf Muffins with Barbecue Sauce*

# Brisket in Ginger Ale

**Serves 8 to 10**

1 (1-liter) bottle ginger ale
3 large onions, sliced
3/4 cup ketchup
1/2 cup chutney
1 envelope onion soup mix
1 envelope mushroom soup mix
5 bay leaves
1 teaspoon peppercorns
1 (5 to 6-pound) beef brisket
Salt and pepper to taste

Preheat the oven to 350 degrees.

Combine the ginger ale, onions, ketchup, chutney, onion soup mix, mushroom soup mix, bay leaves and peppercorns in a roasting pan; mix well.

Season the brisket with salt and pepper and place in the roasting pan. Turn the brisket to coat with sauce. Bake, covered, for 4 hours, turning over the brisket once or twice. Let stand to cool.

Cut the brisket into 1/4-inch slices on a cutting board and transfer to an ovenproof dish. Pour the gravy over the top. Bake at 350 degrees until heated through. Serve immediately.

*Tip: Can be made in advance and frozen. To thaw, place in the refrigerator overnight and then on the counter the morning before serving.*

# Sweet-and-Sour Brisket

**Serves 8**

- 1 (5-pound) beef brisket
- 1 (32-ounce) jar sauerkraut, partially drained
- 1 (28-ounce) can peeled whole tomatoes
- 1 (16-ounce) package brown sugar

Preheat the oven to 350 degrees. Place the brisket in a roasting pan.

Pour the sauerkraut over the brisket. Add the undrained tomatoes. Sprinkle with the brown sugar. Bake, covered, for 3 1/2 hours. Let stand to cool.

Cut the brisket into 1/4-inch slices on a cutting board and return to the sauce. Bake at 350 degrees until heated through and serve.

*Tip:* *See Tip on opposite page.*

# Grilled Skirt Steak

**Serves 3 to 4**

1 (2-pound) skirt steak
1 tablespoon Chef Paul Prudhomme's Magic Seasoning Blends – Meat Magic
1 tablespoon seasoned garlic salt
$^{1}/_{2}$ cup Dale's Steak Seasoning sauce
1 tablespoon vegetable oil (optional)

Season the steak with the seasoning blend and garlic salt. Place in a sealable plastic bag. Add the Dale's sauce. Marinate in the refrigerator for 2 to 3 hours.

Preheat a gas grill or cast-iron skillet. Add the vegetable oil if using a skillet. Grill for 3 to 4 minutes per side. Remove to a cutting board. Let stand for 5 minutes; slice. Serve with salads and baked potatoes.

*Tip: Slice meat thinly against the grain. First, find the direction of the grain (which way the muscle fibers are aligned) and then slice across the grain rather than parallel with it.*

# Meat Loaf Muffins with Barbecue Sauce

**Serves 16**

Vegetable oil or olive oil
2 pounds ground meat, any kind
1 medium onion, cut into chunks
2 ribs celery, cut into 2-inch pieces
1 large egg
1 tablespoon milk
1 cup bread crumbs
2 tablespoons barbecue seasoning
3/4 cup salsa
1 tablespoon Worcestershire sauce
1 tablespoon salt
Favorite barbecue sauce

Preheat the oven to 450 degrees. Brush 16 muffin cups with vegetable oil.

Place the ground meat in a large bowl. Pulse the onion and celery into small pieces in a food processor. Add to the meat.

Beat the egg and milk in a small bowl. Add the egg mixture, bread crumbs and barbecue seasoning to the meat mixture.

Mix the salsa, Worcestershire sauce and salt in a small bowl. Add the salsa mixture to the meat mixture and mix well.

Fill each muffin cup with meat mixture using a scoop. Top each muffin with about 2 teaspoons barbecue sauce. Bake for 20 minutes. Heat additional barbecue sauce to serve on the side.

*pictured on page 65*

# Chinese Meatballs

**Serves 4**

1 pound ground meat, any kind
1 egg
2 tablespoons grated onion
1 tablespoon cornstarch
1 teaspoon ground ginger
Salt and pepper to taste
1 large can pineapple chunks
1 tablespoon vegetable oil
6 tablespoons water
3 tablespoons red wine vinegar
3 tablespoons cornstarch
$^1/_2$ cup sugar
1 tablespoon soy sauce

Preheat the oven to 350 degrees.

Combine the ground meat, egg, onion, cornstarch, ginger, salt and pepper in a large bowl and mix well. Shape into small meatballs. Fry in a skillet until browned and cooked through; drain well. Arrange in a 9×13-inch baking dish.

Drain the pineapple, reserving the juice. Cook the pineapple juice and vegetable oil in a saucepan over low heat for 5 minutes, stirring frequently.

Combine the water, vinegar and cornstarch in a bowl and stir to make a paste. Add the sugar and soy sauce and mix well.

Add the sugar mixture to the pineapple juice mixture. Cook for 10 minutes, stirring occasionally.

Pour the sauce over the meatballs. Spoon the pineapple over the top. Bake for 20 minutes.

# Rack of Lamb

**Serves 4 (2 chops per person)**

**1 rack of lamb**
**1/4 cup olive oil**
**1 teaspoon mixed herbs**
**1 teaspoon rosemary**
**1 teaspoon barbecue seasoning**
**2 tablespoons fresh lemon juice**
**1/2 teaspoon salt**
**1/2 teaspoon pepper**

Preheat the oven to 400 degrees. Place the lamb in a greased foil pan.

Combine the olive oil, mixed herbs, rosemary, barbecue seasoning, lemon juice, salt and pepper in a bowl and mix well. Pour evenly over the lamb.

Bake lamb for 8 to 10 minutes per side. Let stand to rest for 5 minutes. Cut into individual chops.

*Tip: Serve with Grilled Vegetables (recipe on page 104) and a salad of butter lettuce, cherry tomatoes and sliced cucumbers.*

# Grilled Lamb Chops with Mint Pesto

Serves 4

1 bunch fresh mint, chopped
1/4 cup olive oil
2 tablespoons finely chopped walnuts
4 garlic cloves, minced
4 lamb loin chops

Process the mint, olive oil, walnuts and garlic in a small food processor until well blended to make mint pesto.

Baste the lamb chops with the mint pesto. Grill on a barbecue for 4 to 5 minutes per side for medium or to desired degree of doneness, turning and basting with the sauce occasionally. Remove to individual serving plates or to a platter. Garnish with mint sprigs. Serve immediately.

# Veal Marsala

**Serves 4**

1 1/2 pounds veal scallopini
1/2 cup plus 2 tablespoons all-purpose flour
1/4 cup extra-virgin olive oil
4 tablespoons butter
1 large shallot, chopped
8 ounces baby portobello mushrooms or sliced mushrooms
Salt and pepper to taste
1 cup marsala
1 cup beef broth

Coat the veal lightly with 1/2 cup flour. Fry in batches with portions of the olive oil and butter in a skillet for 2 minutes per side, removing to a serving platter.

Combine the shallot and mushrooms in the skillet. Season with salt and pepper. Sauté for 5 minutes. Add the marsala and beef broth. Cook for 2 minutes, stirring constantly and scraping up any browned bits from the bottom of the skillet. Add an additional tablespoon of butter and cook until the butter is melted, stirring constantly. Stir in the remaining flour to thicken the sauce. Spoon the sauce over the veal.

*Tip: May serve over a bed of pasta.*

*Apricot Chicken*

# Poultry

# Chicken Creole

**Serves 6**

1 tablespoon olive oil
1 green bell pepper, minced
1 onion, thinly sliced
1 rib celery
1 garlic clove, minced
2 (16-ounce) cans diced tomatoes
1 bay leaf
1/2 teaspoon salt
1/8 teaspoon cayenne pepper
6 boneless skinless chicken breasts

Preheat the oven to 350 degrees.

Heat the olive oil in a large skillet over medium heat. Add the bell pepper, onion, celery and garlic. Cook for 4 minutes or until the vegetables are tender, stirring occasionally.

Add the undrained tomatoes, bay leaf, salt and cayenne pepper. Cook the creole sauce for 3 minutes, stirring occasionally.

Arrange the chicken in a greased 8×11-inch baking dish. Pour the creole sauce over the chicken. Bake, covered with foil, for 25 minutes or until the chicken is tender and cooked through.

# Chicken Marengo

**Serves 8**

8 boneless skinless chicken breasts
Salt and pepper to taste
All-purpose flour
Vegetable oil
2 onions, chopped
2 garlic cloves, minced
24 ounces beef broth
1 (28-ounce) can crushed tomatoes
1 cup white wine
1 teaspoon dried thyme
Salt and pepper to taste
1 (8-ounce) package sliced fresh mushrooms
1 tablespoon (heaping) cornstarch
1/4 cup cold water

Preheat the oven to 350 degrees.

Season chicken with salt and pepper and coat with flour. Pour enough vegetable oil into a skillet to cover the bottom. Heat over medium-high heat. Cook the chicken in the hot oil for 3 minutes per side or until lightly browned. Remove to a baking dish.

Sauté the onions and garlic with 2 tablespoons of hot vegetable oil in a large skillet until browned. Add the beef broth to the onion mixture. Stir in the tomatoes, wine, thyme, salt and pepper. Bring to a boil. Simmer over low heat for 30 minutes.

Sauté the mushrooms in a small saucepan until tender and any liquid is released and evaporated. Add to the tomato mixture.

Combine the cornstarch and 1/4 cup water in a small bowl and stir until smooth. Add to the sauce and mix well.

Spoon the sauce over the chicken. Bake, covered with foil, for 30 minutes or until the chicken is cooked through.

# Chicken Schnitzel

Serves 8

- 8 boneless skinless chicken breasts
- 3/4 (16-ounce) bottle Italian dressing
- Olive oil spray
- 2 cups crushed cornflakes
- 1/2 cup sesame seeds
- 2 packets onion soup mix

Place the chicken in a large dish. Pour the Italian dressing over the chicken and turn to coat. Marinate, covered, in the refrigerator for 6 hours to overnight.

Preheat the oven to 350 degrees. Spray a large baking sheet or aluminum pan with olive oil spray.

Combine the cornflakes, sesame seeds and onion soup mix in a shallow dish and mix well. Remove the chicken from the marinade and coat with the cornflake mixture. Arrange on the prepared baking sheet. Cover the chicken with plastic wrap and refrigerate for 30 minutes. Remove plastic wrap. Bake for 10 to 15 minutes per side.

Increase the oven temperature to 400 degrees. Bake the chicken for 5 minutes per side, spraying with additional olive oil spray if the chicken appears dry.

# Savory Stuffed Chicken Breasts

**Serves 4**

4 boneless skinless chicken breasts
1/2 cup white wine
1/4 cup orange juice
1 tablespoon prepared mustard
1 teaspoon dried tarragon
4 ounces fresh spinach, stems removed, chopped
4 ounces goat cheese or cream cheese, softened
1/2 cup black Greek olives, chopped
1 teaspoon dried mint
1/2 cup chopped dried apricots

Pound the chicken in a sealable plastic bag using a meat mallet or pot. Combine the wine, orange juice, mustard and tarragon in a baking dish and mix well. Add the chicken to the wine mixture. Marinate for 30 minutes.

Preheat the oven to 325 degrees.

Remove the chicken from the marinade to a work surface, reserving the marinade. Place a fourth of the spinach on the center of each chicken breast.

Combine the cheese, olives, mint and dried apricots in a small bowl and mix well. Divide the mixture among the chicken breasts. Roll up each chicken breast and secure with a toothpick.

Return the chicken to the reserved marinade. Bake for 40 minutes or until cooked through and firm.

# Chutney Chicken

Serves 4 or 5

- 8 chicken pieces
- 1 cup chutney
- 2 tablespoons lemon juice
- 2 teaspoons vegetable oil
- 1 tablespoon sugar
- 1 teaspoon mild or medium curry powder
- 1 teaspoon ground ginger

Preheat the oven to 375 degrees. Arrange the chicken in a greased baking dish.

Combine the chutney, lemon juice, vegetable oil, sugar, curry powder and ginger in a small bowl and mix well. Pour over the chicken.

Bake the chicken for 1 to 1 1/2 hours or until cooked through and browned, turning once; do not overcook.

Tip: *This bone-in chicken is very tasty and succulent, but you can use boneless skinless chicken breasts and reduce the cooking time to 30 minutes.*

# Chicken Drumettes

Serves 8

- 3 (1 1/2-pound) packages chicken drumettes
- 1 cup light soy sauce
- 1 cup water
- 1 cup packed brown sugar

Preheat the oven to 400 degrees.

Arrange the chicken in a baking dish. Combine the soy sauce, water and brown sugar in a bowl and mix well. Pour over the chicken.

Bake, covered with foil, for 30 minutes. Turn over the chicken. Bake, uncovered, for 1 hour or until brown and sticky.

Tip: *Drumettes work well as an appetizer for a sport-watching party.*

# Apricot Chicken

**Serves 4 to 6**

2 tablespoons olive oil
2 pounds chicken tenders, cut
diagonally into halves
Salt and pepper to taste
1 large onion, chopped
2 tablespoons white wine vinegar
12 dried apricots, chopped
2 cups chicken broth
1 cup apricot preserves
Hot cooked rice

Heat a large skillet with a lid over medium heat. Add the olive oil and chicken. Season the chicken with salt and pepper. Cook for 2 to 3 minutes per side or until browned.

Add the onion to the chicken. Cook for 5 minutes, stirring occasionally. Stir in the vinegar and cook until the liquid is evaporated. Add the dried apricots and chicken broth and cook just until bubbly. Stir in the apricot preserves.

Cook, covered, over low heat for 10 to 15 minutes. Spoon over rice. Garnish with chopped fresh parsley.

*pictured on page 76*

# Asian Noodles with Chicken and Pineapple

**Serves 4**

6 ounces green beans, trimmed and cut into halves
1 red bell pepper, chopped
8 ounces rice noodles
1/2 cup fresh lime juice
1/4 cup soy sauce
1 tablespoon sugar
1 pound cooked boneless skinless chicken breasts
1/2 cup fresh or drained canned pineapple chunks
1/4 cup chopped fresh mint
1/2 cup chopped peanuts

Cook the green beans in boiling water in a large pot for 3 minutes. Remove using a slotted spoon. Cook the bell pepper in the water for 5 minutes and remove. Cook the noodles in the water for 4 to 6 minutes or until al dente. Drain the noodles; rinse thoroughly with cold water and drain again.

Whisk the lime juice, soy sauce and sugar in a large bowl until well mixed. Add the vegetables, noodles, chicken, pineapple, mint and peanuts and toss to coat. Serve immediately.

*Tip: Al dente means cooked so as to be still firm when bitten.*

# Chicken Piccata Pasta Toss

**Serves 8 to 10**

4 tablespoons olive oil
1 1/4 pounds chicken tenders,
cut into halves
Salt and pepper to taste
2 medium shallots, chopped
4 garlic cloves, chopped
2 tablespoons all-purpose flour
1/2 cup white wine
Juice of 1 lemon
1 cup chicken broth
3 tablespoons capers
1/2 cup chopped fresh parsley
12 ounces penne pasta

Heat a deep nonstick skillet over medium-high heat. Add 2 tablespoons olive oil and chicken. Season the chicken with salt and pepper. Cook for 2 to 3 minutes per side or until light golden brown. Remove the chicken to a serving dish.

Add 2 tablespoons olive oil, shallots and garlic to the skillet. Sauté for 3 minutes. Reduce the heat to medium. Stir in the flour and cook for 2 minutes. Whisk in the wine and cook for 1 minute to reduce the liquid. Whisk in the lemon juice and chicken broth. Stir in the capers and parsley. Bring to a low boil. Return the chicken to the skillet. Cook until heated through.

Meanwhile, cook the pasta until al dente; drain. Combine the hot pasta and chicken with sauce in the serving dish and toss to mix.

*Tip: Microwave hard lemons for 30 seconds to release the juices.*

# Chicken Lettuce Wraps

**Serves 4**

1 head butter lettuce
1 small white onion, chopped
3 green onions, sliced
1/4 cup olive oil
1 pound ground chicken or turkey
1/2 cup soy sauce
2 tablespoons brown sugar
1 tablespoon oyster sauce
1 teaspoon chopped garlic
1 teaspoon dried or chopped fresh ginger
1/16 teaspoon red pepper flakes
1 cup canned chow mein noodles or bean sprouts
1/2 cup pine nuts

Separate the lettuce leaves carefully to create lettuce cups, trimming any tough ends; rinse and dry thoroughly.

Sauté the white onion and green onions with the olive oil in a skillet until tender. Add the ground chicken and cook until browned, stirring to crumble; drain.

Add the soy sauce, brown sugar, oyster sauce, garlic, ginger and red pepper flakes to the chicken mixture and mix well. Stir in the chow mein noodles and pine nuts.

Serve immediately in the lettuce cups, garnishing with additional chow mein noodles.

*Tip: These wraps can be served as an appetizer for 8 people.*

# Barbecue Chicken Pizza

Serves 6

8 ounces chopped cooked chicken
2/3 cup favorite barbecue sauce
1 can ready-made pizza dough
3/4 cup shredded mild cheddar cheese
1 cup shredded mozzarella cheese
3/4 cup parmesan cheese
1/4 medium red onion, thinly sliced

Preheat the oven to 350 degrees. Spray a baking sheet with nonstick cooking spray.

Place the chicken in a bowl. Add a small amount of barbecue sauce and toss to coat.

Press the dough into a 10×15-inch rectangle on the prepared baking sheet. Spread with the remaining barbecue sauce. Top with the cheeses, onion and chicken.

Bake the pizza for 20 minutes. Garnish with chopped fresh parsley. Cut into pieces and serve.

Tip: *Purchase a rotisserie chicken or use leftover grilled or baked chicken breasts. If short on time, buy a premade pizza crust.*

# Harvest Turkey Burgers

Serves 4

1 pound ground turkey
1/2 red bell pepper, chopped
1 carrot, shredded (about 1/2 cup)
2 scallions, finely chopped
2 tablespoons chopped fresh, or 2 teaspoons dried thyme
Coarse salt and freshly ground pepper to taste
Olive oil
4 hamburger buns, split
4 lettuce leaves
1 tomato, sliced
Ranch or herb dressing

Combine the ground turkey, bell pepper, carrot, scallions, thyme, salt and pepper in a bowl and mix well. Shape into 4 patties and brush both sides with olive oil.

Cook in a heated nonstick skillet or grill on a barbecue for 7 minutes per side. Serve in the buns with tomato, lettuce and dressing.

*Tilapia with a Tasty Topping*

# Seafood

# Baked Salmon in Orange Juice

**Serves 10**

**1 (2 1/2-pound) whole side salmon, skin removed**
**Orange juice**
**1/4 cup honey**
**1/4 cup soy sauce**

Preheat the oven to 500 degrees. Spray a large aluminum pan with nonstick cooking spray.

Place the salmon in the prepared pan. Add orange juice to a depth of 1/2 inch. Drizzle the honey and soy sauce over the salmon.

Bake for 20 minutes or until browned, watching carefully. Garnish with orange slices and chopped fresh parsley.

# Asian Salmon

**Serves 10 to 12**

**Olive oil spray**
**1 (3-pound) whole side salmon**
**6 tablespoons olive oil**
**3 tablespoons soy sauce**
**2 tablespoons dijon mustard**
**1/2 garlic clove, minced**

Preheat the oven to 400 degrees. Line a large baking sheet with foil. Spray the foil with olive oil spray.

Place the salmon skin side down on the prepared baking sheet. Combine the olive oil, soy sauce, mustard and garlic in a small bowl and whisk to mix. Drizzle half the marinade over the salmon. Let stand for 10 minutes.

Broil the salmon for 20 minutes. Remove to a plate. Drizzle with the reserved marinade. Let stand for 10 minutes. Serve warm, at room temperature or chilled.

# Rigatoni

**Serves 8**

Olive oil spray
1 (16-ounce) can tomato purée
1 (16-ounce) can whole tomatoes
1 cup heavy cream (optional)
1 tablespoon Italian seasoning
1 tablespoon dried basil
1 tablespoon dried oregano
Salt and pepper to taste
2 (5-ounce) cans salmon, drained
1 (1-pound) box rigatoni
1/2 cup grated parmesan cheese
1 cup shredded mozzarella cheese

Preheat the oven to 350 degrees. Spray a 9×13-inch baking dish with olive oil spray.

Combine the tomato purée, whole tomatoes, cream, Italian seasoning, basil, oregano, salt and pepper in a saucepan. Bring to a boil. Simmer for 45 minutes or until the sauce is slightly reduced and rich in color.

Flake the salmon with a fork. Add to the sauce and stir gently.

Cook the rigatoni according to the package directions just until al dente; drain.

Layer the rigatoni, salmon mixture, parmesan cheese and mozzarella cheese a third at a time in the prepared baking dish, ending with the mozzarella cheese. Bake for 1 hour.

*Tip: This pasta dish freezes great. Mushrooms or tuna may be used as a substitute for the salmon.*

# Tilapia with a Tasty Topping

**Serves 5**

**1/2 cup mayonnaise**
**1/2 cup grated mild cheddar cheese (optional)**
**2 tablespoons (heaping) dijon mustard**
**2 tablespoons panko bread crumbs**
**1 tablespoon chopped fresh parsley**
**5 (6-ounce) tilapia fillets**
**Salt and pepper to taste**

Preheat the oven to 350 degrees. Spray a baking sheet with nonstick cooking spray.

Combine the mayonnaise, cheese, mustard, bread crumbs and parsley in a bowl and mix well.

Rinse and dry the tilapia. Season with salt and pepper. Arrange on the prepared baking sheet. Spread the tilapia thinly with the mayonnaise mixture. Bake for 15 minutes. Place the fish 6 inches from the heat source and broil for 3 minutes. Garnish servings with lemon slices and chopped fresh parsley.

Tip: *Always spray pans used for cooking or baking with nonstick cooking spray. Food will come out easier, and you can wash the pan without soaking or scrubbing it first.*

*pictured on page 92*

# Shrimp in Garlic Butter Sauce

**Serves 4**

**1/2 cup butter**
**1 1/2 pounds shrimp, peeled and deveined**
**6 garlic cloves, cut into halves**
**1/2 lemon, sliced**
**2 tablespoons chopped green onions**
**2 tablespoons lemon juice**
**Salt and pepper to taste**

Melt the butter in a large saucepan over medium heat. Add the shrimp and garlic. Cook for 5 minutes, in batches if necessary; turn over the shrimp. Add the lemon and green onions. Cook for 5 minutes. Remove and discard the garlic. Stir in the lemon juice, salt and pepper. Serve over rice or pasta.

Tip: *Serve with a salad, and you'll have dinner in just 15 minutes.*

# Sides

Zucchini Pancakes

# Vegetable Bake

**Serves 6 to 8**

1 (14-ounce) can asparagus cuts
1 (8-ounce) can sliced mushrooms, drained
1 (14-ounce) can quartered artichoke, drained
4 tablespoons butter
1/4 cup all-purpose flour
1/2 cup milk
1 tablespoon dijon mustard
Salt and pepper to taste
1 cup shredded sharp cheddar cheese
1/2 cup chopped fresh tomato
1 (2-ounce) can sliced black olives, drained

Preheat the oven to 350 degrees.

Drain the asparagus, reserving the liquid. Combine the asparagus, mushrooms and artichokes in a greased baking dish.

Melt the butter in a saucepan over medium heat. Stir in the flour. Add the milk gradually stirring constantly. Add the reserved asparagus liquid gradually, stirring constantly. Stir in the mustard, salt and pepper. Pour evenly over the vegetables. Sprinkle with the cheese.

Pat the tomatoes dry with a paper towel. Arrange tomatoes and black olives decoratively over the cheese. Bake for 30 minutes.

# Grilled Vegetables

**Serves 6**

**1 bunch asparagus**
**1 cup olive oil**
**3/4 cup balsamic vinegar**
**6 portobello mushrooms**

Tip: *Do not wash mushrooms. Simply wipe off any dirt with a damp paper towel. Mushrooms are like sponges and absorb water, so they will lose flavor if washed with water.*

Preheat the grill.

Cut off and discard the bottom 2 inches of the asparagus. Combine the olive oil and vinegar in a small bowl and mix well. Pour half the marinade over the mushrooms in a bowl. Pour the remaining marinade over the asparagus in a separate bowl. Marinate for 15 minutes.

Arrange the mushrooms on one side of a foil pan. Arrange the asparagus on the other side of the pan. Grill the vegetables for 10 minutes or until the asparagus is crisp and tender. Remove the asparagus to a serving platter. Grill the mushrooms for 5 minutes longer. Remove to the serving platter.

# Herbed Corn and Couscous

**Serves 2**

**1 cup fresh corn kernels or frozen corn, thawed**
**1 tablespoon unsalted butter**
**3/4 cup chicken broth**
**1/2 cup couscous**
**2 tablespoons minced fresh chives**
**Salt and pepper to taste**

Cook the corn in the butter in a small saucepan over medium-high heat for 1 minute, stirring constantly. Add the chicken broth. Bring to a boil. Stir in the couscous.

Remove the couscous from the heat; cover. Let stand for 5 minutes. Stir in the chives, salt and pepper.

# Cheesy Cauliflower

**Serves 3 to 4**

1 large head cauliflower
1 (32-ounce) box chicken or vegetable broth
3 ounces boursin
2 tablespoons chopped fresh chives or dried chives
1/4 teaspoon ground nutmeg
1/2 teaspoon salt
1/2 teaspoon pepper

Remove and discard the cauliflower leaves. Combine the cauliflower and broth in a large pot over high heat; cover. Bring to a boil. Reduce the heat to medium. Cook until the cauliflower is fork tender; drain.

Mash the cauliflower. Add the cheese and mash until well mixed. Stir in the chives, nutmeg, salt and pepper. Spoon into a serving dish.

Tip: *Any soft garlic-and-herb cheese will work in place of the boursin.*

# Potato Kugel

**Serves 4 or 5**

6 medium russet potatoes
1 large onion
2 eggs, beaten
2 tablespoons (heaping) all-purpose flour
2 tablespoons vegetable oil
1 teaspoon baking powder
1 1/2 teaspoons salt
1/8 teaspoon pepper
Olive oil spray

Preheat the oven to 350 degrees. Spray a 6×8-inch baking dish with nonstick cooking spray.

Grate the potatoes and onion in a food processor; drain. Spoon into a bowl. Add the eggs and mix well. Stir in the flour, vegetable oil, baking powder, salt and pepper.

Spoon the potato mixture into the prepared baking dish. Spray with olive oil spray. Bake for 1 to 1 1/2 hours or until browned.

Tip: *The toothpick test is a helpful way to determine if this dish is ready. Simply insert a toothpick three-quarters of the way into the kugel and remove. If the toothpick comes out clean, it's ready.*

# Tomato Vegetable Casserole

**Serves 6 to 8**

- 1 medium potato
- 1 medium yam
- 2 carrots
- 1 red bell pepper
- 1/2 red onion
- 1 large tomato
- 4 tablespoons olive oil plus additional for drizzling
- Salt and pepper to taste
- 1/2 cup grated parmesan cheese
- 2 tablespoons Italian bread crumbs

Preheat the oven to 400 degrees.

Peel the potato, yam and carrots and cut into 1/2-inch pieces. Seed the bell pepper and cut into 1/2-inch pieces. Cut the onion into thin slices and separate into rings. Cut the tomato into 1/4-inch slices.

Combine the potato, yam, bell pepper, carrots and 2 tablespoons olive oil in a 9×12-inch baking dish and toss to coat. Sprinkle with salt and pepper. Spread the vegetables evenly in the baking dish.

Arrange the onion slices evenly over the vegetables. Drizzle with 2 tablespoons olive oil and sprinkle with salt and pepper. Arrange the tomato slices evenly over the vegetables.

Stir the parmesan cheese and bread crumbs in a small bowl. Sprinkle over the vegetables. Drizzle with additional olive oil until moist. Bake for 1 hour or until golden brown.

# Squash Casserole

**Serves 3 or 4**

2 pounds yellow squash, cut into 1/2-inch slices
1 small onion, chopped
1 small green bell pepper, chopped
2 teaspoons olive oil
1 teaspoon salt
1 teaspoon white pepper
1 1/2 pounds shredded medium cheddar cheese
1 cup Italian bread crumbs

Preheat the oven to 350 degrees.

Sauté the squash, onion and bell pepper with the olive oil in a skillet until the squash is tender. Season with the salt and pepper. Stir in the cheese and 1/2 cup bread crumbs. Spoon into a baking dish.

Sprinkle the remaining 1/2 cup bread crumbs over the squash mixture. Bake for 30 minutes or until golden brown.

# Zucchini Pancakes

**Makes 7**

2 cups grated zucchini
Salt to taste
2 eggs, beaten
3 tablespoons butter, melted
1/2 cup grated parmesan cheese
3/4 cup all-purpose flour
Pepper to taste

Sprinkle the zucchini lightly with salt in a strainer over a bowl. Let stand for 30 minutes. Rinse the zucchini and press to squeeze dry.

Combine the zucchini, eggs, butter, cheese, flour, salt and pepper in a bowl and mix well.

Drop the mixture by 2 heaping tablespoons into a lightly buttered pan. Fry for 3 minutes per side or until lightly browned. Keep warm.

*Tip: This recipe doubles easily.*

*pictured on page 101*

# Honeyed Wild Rice with Vegetables

**Serves 6 to 8**

- 1 cup wild rice
- 1/2 cup long grain rice
- 4 tablespoons butter
- 2 small zucchinis, shredded
- 2 small carrots, shredded
- 1 tablespoon honey
- 2 teaspoons soy sauce

Cook the wild rice and long grain rice with water separately according to the package directions.

Heat the butter in a saucepan. Add the zucchinis, carrots and honey. Cook for 2 minutes, stirring constantly.

Combine the wild rice, long grain rice, zucchini mixture and soy sauce in a bowl and toss to mix.

Tip: *If you prefer a sweeter dish, add more honey. If you prefer a more savory dish, add more soy sauce.*

# Desserts

*Pillow Puff Pastry*

# Best-Ever Butter Cake

**Serves 10 to 12**

1 cup butter, softened
2 cups sugar
4 eggs, lightly beaten
3 cups all-purpose flour
4 teaspoons baking powder
1 teaspoon salt
1 cup sour cream
1 teaspoon vanilla extract
Grated zest of 1 lemon or orange
Powdered sugar

Preheat the oven to 350 degrees. Grease a bundt pan and dust with flour.

Cream the butter and sugar in a mixing bowl until light and fluffy. Beat in the eggs.

Sift the flour, baking powder and salt into a bowl. Add to the creamed mixture alternately with the sour cream and vanilla extract, mixing well after each addition. Add the lemon zest and mix until smooth.

Pour the batter into the prepared bundt pan. Bake for 45 to 50 minutes or until the cake tests done. Cool in the pan for 10 minutes. Invert onto a cake plate. Dust with powdered sugar.

*Tip: Test with a skewer after 45 minutes. If the skewer comes out with wet batter, the cake needs more time to bake. If it comes out clean, the cake is done.*

*Variations:* *See page 120.*

# Variations for Best-Ever Butter Cake

## Cherry Cake

Dust 1 cup glacé cherries with a small amount of flour and fold into the Best-Ever Butter Cake batter after adding the lemon zest.

## Cranberry or Currant Cake

Fold 1 cup dried cranberries or currants into the Best-Ever Butter Cake batter after adding the lemon zest.

## Marble Cake

Combine a fourth of the Best-Ever Butter Cake batter with 3 tablespoons sifted baking cocoa and 2 teaspoons milk or black coffee in a bowl and mix well.

Spoon the remaining batter into the prepared bundt pan. Drop the chocolate batter by spoonfuls onto the plain batter and swirl with a knife to create a marble effect.

## Streusel Cake

Combine 1/2 cup chopped walnuts or pecans, 1/2 cup packed brown sugar, 2 tablespoons all-purpose flour, 2 tablespoons melted butter and 1 teaspoon ground cinnamon in a bowl and mix well. Pour half the Best-Ever Butter Cake batter into the prepared bundt pan. Spread half the streusel over the batter. Repeat with the remaining batter and streusel.

## Walnut Cake

Break 1/2 cup walnuts coarsely. Fold the walnuts into the Best-Ever Butter Cake batter after adding the lemon zest.

# Easy Chocolate Cake

**Serves 10**

1 $^1/_2$ cups sugar
2 cups all-purpose flour
$^1/_2$ cup baking cocoa
1 teaspoon instant coffee
1 teaspoon baking powder
1 teaspoon baking soda
1 $^1/_4$ cups milk, water or orange juice
3 eggs
$^3/_4$ cup vegetable oil
Chocolate frosting

*Tip: When cooking, using a little more or a little less of an ingredient is not going to make any difference. When baking, the measurements need to be accurate.*

Preheat the oven to 325 degrees. Grease a bundt pan generously.

Process the sugar, flour, baking cocoa, instant coffee, baking powder and baking soda in a food processor fitted with a steel blade for 10 seconds or until blended. Add the milk and eggs and process until smooth. Add the oil in a fine stream, processing constantly. Process the batter for 45 seconds or until smooth; do not insert the pusher into the feed tube and do not overprocess.

Pour the batter into the prepared bundt pan. Bake for 1 hour or until the cake tests done. Cool in the pan for 20 minutes. Invert onto a cake plate. Spread with your favorite chocolate frosting. This cake freezes well.

# Molten Chocolate Cakes

**Serves 6**

1 cup baking cocoa
10 tablespoons unsalted butter
3 large eggs
3 egg yolks
$1^1/2$ cups powdered sugar
$^1/2$ cup all-purpose flour

Preheat the oven to 450 degrees. Spray six $3^1/2$-inch ramekins with nonstick cooking spray.

Combine the baking cocoa and butter in a saucepan. Cook over low heat until the butter is melted, stirring constantly. Let stand to cool slightly.

Combine the eggs and egg yolks in a large bowl and whisk until blended. Whisk in the powdered sugar, cocoa mixture and flour. Divide evenly among the prepared ramekins.

Bake for 11 minutes or until the sides of the cakes are set but the centers remain soft and runny. Loosen the cake from the sides of the ramekins using a small knife. Invert onto serving plates. Serve with vanilla ice cream or fresh berries.

*Tip: The cake batter can be prepared ahead of time, poured into the ramekins and refrigerated. Let stand at room temperature for 30 minutes before baking.*

# Apple Cake

Serves 10

- 2 cups plus 2 tablespoons sugar
- 2 cups all-purpose flour
- 3 Granny Smith apples, peeled and cut into 1-inch pieces
- 1 cup vegetable oil
- 2 eggs, beaten until foamy
- 1 teaspoon ground cinnamon
- 1/2 teaspoon salt
- 1 teaspoon baking soda
- 1 teaspoon vanilla extract

Preheat the oven to 350 degrees. Grease a bundt pan. Sprinkle 2 tablespoons sugar into the pan and swirl to coat the sides.

Combine the flour, 2 cups sugar, apples, vegetable oil, eggs, cinnamon salt, baking soda and vanilla extract in a large bowl and mix well. Spoon into the prepared bundt pan.

Bake for 1 hour. Let stand to cool. Invert onto a cake plate.

# Key Lime Pie

Serves 10 to 12

- 1 1/2 cups graham cracker crumbs
- 1/2 cup sugar
- 4 tablespoons butter, melted
- 2 (14-ounce) cans sweetened condensed milk
- 1 cup lime juice
- 2 eggs
- 1 cup sour cream
- 2 tablespoons powdered sugar
- 1 tablespoon lime zest

Preheat the oven to 375 degrees.

Combine the graham cracker crumbs, sugar and butter in a bowl and mix well using hands. Press over the bottom and up the side of a 9-inch pie plate. Bake for 20 minutes. Let stand to cool.

Combine the condensed milk, lime juice and eggs in a bowl and whisk until well blended. Pour into the graham cracker crust. Bake for 15 minutes. Chill, covered, for 2 hours or longer.

Combine the sour cream and powdered sugar in a bowl and mix well. Spread over the top of the pie. Sprinkle with the lime zest. Chill until serving time.

# Brandy Tart

Serves 10 to 12

1 cup chopped dates
1 cup boiling water
1 teaspoon baking soda
1 cup sugar
1 egg
$2\frac{1}{2}$ tablespoons butter
$1\frac{1}{4}$ cups all-purpose flour
2 teaspoons baking powder
$\frac{1}{4}$ teaspoon salt
1 cup chopped walnuts
Syrup

Preheat the oven to 375 degrees. Butter a tart pan or large pie plate.

Combine the dates, boiling water and baking soda in a bowl and mix well.

Process the sugar, egg and butter in a food processor until creamy. Add the flour, baking powder and salt and process to mix well. Add the date mixture and process to mix well. Stir in the walnuts. Pour into the prepared pan. Bake for 20 to 30 minutes or until set.

Let the tart cool slightly. Pour the Syrup over the top. Let stand for 10 minutes, allowing the syrup to seep into the tart.

## Syrup

$1\frac{1}{4}$ cups sugar
$\frac{3}{4}$ cup water
$\frac{1}{4}$ cup brandy
1 tablespoon butter

### For the Syrup

Combine the sugar and water in a small saucepan. Bring to a boil. Boil for 5 minutes, stirring occasionally. Stir in the brandy and butter. Let stand to cool.

*Tip: Can be made in advance. Cover with plastic wrap and refrigerate. Remove plastic wrap and warm at 300 degrees for 10 minutes. Serve with vanilla ice cream or whipped cream.*

# Ginger Peach Cobbler

**Serves 6**

- 2 (14-ounce) cans sliced peaches in syrup, drained
- 1 tablespoon ground ginger
- 1/4 cup packed brown sugar
- 2 tablespoons butter, softened
- 1 cup granola with raisins and nuts
- 2 egg whites, beaten

Preheat the oven to 400 degrees.

Combine the peaches and ginger in a bowl and mix well. Divide the mixture evenly among six 3-inch ovenproof ramekins.

Combine the brown sugar and butter in a bowl and mix with a fork. Add the granola and mix well. Fold in the egg whites.

Divide the granola mixture evenly among the ramekins. Place the ramekins on a baking sheet. Bake for 10 to 12 minutes. Let stand to cool slightly. Serve warm or at room temperature with vanilla ice cream.

*Tip: If you don't have ramekins, you can use a 9-inch pie plate and bake for 20 minutes.*

# Cheesecake

**Serves 10**

**2 1/2 cups graham cracker crumbs**
**1/2 cup butter, melted**
**3 eggs**
**1/2 cup sugar**
**16 ounces cream cheese, softened**
**1 tablespoon all-purpose flour**
**1 cup whipped cream**

Preheat the oven to 300 degrees.

Combine the graham cracker crumbs and butter in a bowl and mix well. Press over the bottom of a 9-inch pie plate. Place in the refrigerator while making filling.

Beat the eggs and sugar in a mixing bowl. Beat in the cream cheese and flour. Fold in the whipped cream.

Pour the cream cheese mixture over the graham cracker crust. Bake for 45 minutes or until set.

# Chocolate Mousse

Serves 4 to 5

1 teaspoon unflavored gelatin
1/4 cup cold water
1/4 cup boiling water
4 ounces bitter chocolate
1 teaspoon vanilla extract
4 eggs yolks
1/3 cup sugar
4 egg whites, beaten
1 cup heavy cream, beaten

Soften the gelatin in the cold water in a small bowl. Add the boiling water and stir until dissolved.

Melt the chocolate in a double boiler without stirring. Remove from the heat. Add the vanilla extract and gelatin and mix well.

Beat the egg yolks and sugar in a mixing bowl until thick and creamy. Add the chocolate mixture, beating constantly.

Fold the egg whites into the chocolate mixture. Fold in the beaten cream.

Pour the mousse into a 3-cup glass dish. Chill for 3 to 4 hours or overnight. Garnish with grated chocolate.

*Tip: If you don't have a double boiler, place a saucepan on the stove and fill halfway with water. Bring to a simmer. Place a glass bowl on top of the saucepan. Add the chocolate and stir until melted.*

# Fruit Florentines

**Yields 50**

**3 to 4 boxes miniature phyllo shells (50 shells)**
**8 ounces dark or milk chocolate, melted**
**2 cups cornflakes**
**1 cup glacé mixed fruit**
**1 cup chopped pecans**
**12 ounces sweetened condensed milk**
**Pecan halves or glacé cherries**

Arrange the phyllo shells on a baking sheet. Divide the chocolate evenly among the phyllo shells. Refrigerate for 10 minutes or until the chocolate has hardened.

Preheat the oven to 350 degrees.

Combine the cornflakes, mixed fruit, pecans and condensed milk in a bowl and mix well. Divide evenly among the prepared shells. Top each with half a glacé cherry or a pecan half. Bake for 15 minutes.

*Tip: Florentines are the perfect dessert to make ahead of time and store in plastic containers in the freezer. Remove 30 minutes before serving.*

# Mandarin Pudding

Serves 8 to 10

3 (3-ounce) packages orange gelatin
$1\frac{1}{2}$ cups boiling water
1 (12-ounce) can frozen orange juice concentrate, thawed
3 (11-ounce) cans mandarin oranges in juice
11 ice cubes

Combine the gelatin and water in a bowl and stir until the gelatin is dissolved. Add the orange juice concentrate and mix well.

Drain the mandarin oranges, reserving the juice. Add the mandarin orange juice to the gelatin mixture. Add the ice cubes and stir until melted. Stir in the mandarin oranges. Chill overnight to set.

*Tip: These look great presented in shot glasses, serving 24.*

# Pillow Puff Pastry

**Serves 6 to 8**

2 frozen puff pastry sheets, thawed in the refrigerator
2 (3-ounce) packages instant vanilla pudding mix
4 cups cold milk
1 cup powdered sugar
$1\frac{1}{2}$ tablespoons water
8 ounces semi-sweet chocolate

Preheat the oven to 350 degrees.

Unroll the pastry sheets and place each sheet on a 9×13-inch baking sheet. Bake for 30 minutes. Let stand to cool.

Prepare the vanilla pudding with the milk according to the package directions. Chill until set.

Place one of the pastry sheets on a platter. Spread the vanilla pudding over the pastry. Place the remaining pastry sheet over the vanilla pudding, making a sandwich.

Mix the powdered sugar with the water in a bowl to make icing. Melt the chocolate in a bowl in the microwave. Drizzle the icing and chocolate alternately over the pastry. Chill until serving time.

*Tip: Any pudding filling, like chocolate or butterscotch, will work with this recipe.*

*pictured on page 116*

# Tiramisu

**Serves 8**

6 tablespoons instant espresso
3 tablespoons boiling water
1 1/2 cups cold water
8 ounces cream cheese
3/4 cup heavy cream
1/3 cup sugar
2 (3-ounce) packages soft ladyfingers
Baking cocoa for dusting

Combine the espresso and boiling water in a bowl and stir until the espresso is dissolved. Add the cold water and stir.

Beat the cream cheese, heavy cream and sugar in a mixing bowl until light and fluffy. Spread a few tablespoons of the cream cheese mixture over the bottom of an 8×8-inch serving dish.

Dip a third of the ladyfingers into the espresso mixture and arrange over the cream cheese. Spread a third of the remaining cream cheese mixture over the ladyfingers. Alternate layers of ladyfingers dipped in the espresso mixture and the cream cheese mixture 2 more times, ending with the cream cheese mixture. Dust with the baking cocoa. Refrigerate for up to 1 day.

# Piña Glace

**Serves 8 to 10**

- 1 (3-ounce) package pineapple gelatin
- 1 cup boiling water
- 1 (1-pint) container vanilla ice cream
- 1 (15-ounce) can crushed pineapple, drained

Dissolve the gelatin in the water in a large bowl. Stir in the ice cream and pineapple. Pour into a serving bowl and chill overnight.

*Tip: This recipe doubles easily.*

# Soft Meringue

**Serves 10 to 12**

6 egg whites
1/4 teaspoon cream of tartar
1 1/2 cups sugar
1 1/2 teaspoons lemon juice
1 1/2 teaspoons cornstarch
1/2 teaspoon vanilla extract
Whipped cream
Mixed berries and sliced kiwi

Preheat the oven to 450 degrees. Line a baking sheet with parchment paper.

Beat the egg whites with the cream of tartar at high speed in a mixing bowl until soft peaks form. Add the sugar gradually, beating until shiny stiff peaks form. Beat in the lemon juice, cornstarch and vanilla extract. Spread the meringue 1/2 inch thick on the prepared baking sheet.

Reduce the oven temperature to 250 degrees. Bake the meringue for 20 minutes. Reduce the oven temperature to 200 degrees. Bake for 1 hour. Let stand to cool.

Spread whipped cream over the meringue Arrange berries and kiwi over the top. Serve immediately.

*Tip: Meringue is best baked and eaten on the same day. Topping should be placed on meringue within 1 hour of serving.*

# *Settings Simplified*

A beautiful table is truly a work of art, expressing everything from the setter's mood to a specific theme, season, or holiday. Creativity is more important than perfection when thinking through your table setting. Whether you're using everyday plates or heirloom china, you can find inspiration anywhere to match the menu you have created for the evening.

# Table Settings for Two

# Table Settings for Four

# Table Settings for Six

# Menu Suggestions for Two

ARTICHOKE SPINACH DIP 35

Served with crackers

CABBAGE AND TOMATO SLAW WITH SHERRY VINAIGRETTE 47

APRICOT CHICKEN 84

HONEYED WILD RICE WITH VEGETABLES 114

PIÑA GLACE 135

# Menu Suggestions for Two

Baked Brie with Chutney 28

Served with sliced vegetables, apples and baguette

Lobster Bisque 56

Rack of Lamb 71

Potato Kugel 108

Cheesecake 128

Avocado Dip 36

Served with potato chips, carrot sticks, sliced mushrooms, radishes and/or celery sticks

Spinach Salad with Apricot Vinaigrette 46

Asian Salmon 96

Rigatoni 97

(omit salmon in recipe)

Chocolate Mousse 129

# Menu Suggestions for Four

BAKED CRAB DIP 26

Served with sliced fresh vegetables

BUTTERNUT SQUASH SOUP 61

Served with rolls or baguette slices

CHICKEN PICCATA PASTA TOSS 86

CABBAGE SALAD 49

APPLE CAKE 124

Served with Vanilla Ice Cream or Whipped Cream

# Menu Suggestions for Four

Skinny Chopped Vegetable Salad 51

Vegetable Soup 57

Tilapia with a Tasty Topping 98

or

Meat Loaf Muffins
with Barbecue Sauce 69

Served with roasted potatoes

Mandarin Pudding 132

Before-dinner drinks

Served on a pretty tray

Pesto Torta 30

Served with baguette slices and crudités

Brisket in Ginger Ale 66

Squash Casserole 112

or

Tomato Vegetable Casserole 111

Best-Ever Butter Cake 118

and/or

Key Lime Pie 124

# Menu Suggestions for Six

Salmon Mousse 26

Served with crackers or cocktail rye bread
and before-dinner drinks

Tomato, Mozzarella and Basil Salad 52

Pass balsamic vinegar and olive oil

Chicken Marengo 79

Served over pasta or rice

Zucchini Pancakes 113

Molten Chocolate Cakes 123

Served with fresh berries

# Menu Suggestions for Six

STUFFED LOAF WITH ASPARAGUS AND MUSHROOMS 32

FRESH MUSHROOM SOUP 60

or

SPINACH SALAD WITH POPPY SEED DRESSING 44

BAKED SALMON IN ORANGE JUICE 94

HERBED CORN AND COUSCOUS 105

and/or

VEGETABLE BAKE 102

FRUIT FLORENTINES 130

Served with coffee

# Index

Special thanks to the following individuals for their contributions to the development of this book:

Writing and Project Management
Shelby Tuttle
Joanne Yurich

Photography Credits
Book Interior: Rebecca White
Back Cover: Dave Shafer Photography

Phone number: 972.248.8510
Website: www.startingfromscratchcooking.com



ISBN: 978-0-87197-643-7
Library of Congress Control Number: 2017900731
Printed in China
10 9 8 7 6 5 4 3 2 1

Favorite Recipes® Press

*Starting from Scratch* was edited, designed, and manufactured by Favorite Recipes Press in collaboration with Merle Rosenbloom Enterprises LLC. Favorite Recipes Press works with top chefs, food and appliance manufacturers, restaurants and resorts, health organizations, Junior Leagues, and nonprofit organizations to create award-winning cookbooks and other food-related products. Favorite Recipes Press is an imprint of Southwestern Publishing Group, Inc., 2451 Atrium Way, Nashville, Tennessee 37214. Southwestern Publishing Group is a wholly owned subsidiary of Southwestern/Great American, Inc., Nashville, Tennessee.

Christopher G. Capen, President,
Southwestern Publishing Group
Sheila Thomas, Publisher,
Favorite Recipes Press
Kristin Connelly, Managing Editor
Steve Newman, Designer
Linda Brock, Editor
Rhonda Brock, Proofreader
www.frpbooks.com | 800.358.0560